SHARIA:
THE THREAT TO AMERICA

ABRIDGED

Center for Security Policy Press
© 2016

This book may be reproduced, distributed and
transmitted for personal or non-commercial use.
Contact the Center for Security Policy for bulk order information.

Copyright © 2016 Center for Security Policy

Sharia: The Threat to America: Abridged is published in the
United States by the Center for Security Policy Press,
a division of the Center for Security Policy.

THE CENTER FOR SECURITY POLICY
1901 Pennsylvania Avenue, Suite 201
Washington, DC 20006
Phone: (202) 835-9077

Email: info@securefreedom.org
For more information, please see securefreedom.org

ISBN-13: 978-1535032292
ISBN-10: 1535032294

Book design by Adam Savit
Cover design by J.P. Zarruk

CONTENTS

- CONTENTS 3
- TEAM B II MEMBERS 5
- FOREWORD 9
- EXECUTIVE SUMMARY 11
  - THE THREAT IS SHARIA 11
  - MISPERCEIVING THE THREAT 13
  - THE MUSLIM BROTHERHOOD 14
  - THE WELLSPRING OF JIHAD 17
  - A NEEDED REALITY CHECK 18
  - THE ENEMY WITHIN 20
  - THE TACIT SUPPORTERS OF CIVILIZATION JIHAD 22
  - THE NEED FOR CORRECTIVE ACTION 24
  - RECOMMENDATIONS 27
- KEY FINDINGS 31
- KEY TENETS OF SHARIA 35
- REFERENCES 47

MEMBERS OF TEAM B II

Team Leaders

LIEUTENANT GENERAL WILLIAM G. "JERRY" BOYKIN

US Army (Ret.), former Deputy Undersecretary of Defense for Intelligence

LIEUTENANT GENERAL HARRY EDWARD SOYSTER

US Army (Ret.), former Director, Defense Intelligence Agency

Associates

CHRISTINE BRIM

Chief Operating Officer, Center for Security Policy

AMBASSADOR HENRY COOPER

former Chief Negotiator, Defense and Space Talks, former Director, Strategic Defense Initiative

STEPHEN C. COUGHLIN, ESQ.

Major (Res.) USA, former Senior Consultant, Office of the Joint Chiefs of Staff

MICHAEL DEL ROSSO

Senior Fellow, Claremont Institute and Center for Security Policy

FRANK J. GAFFNEY, JR.

former Assistant Secretary of Defense for International Security Policy (Acting), President, Center for Security Policy

JOHN GUANDOLO

former Special Agent, Counter-Terrorism Division, Federal Bureau of Investigation

BRIAN KENNEDY

President, Claremont Institute

CLARE M. LOPEZ

Senior Fellow, Center for Security Policy

ADMIRAL JAMES A. "ACE" LYONS

US Navy (Ret.), former Commander-in-Chief, Pacific Fleet

ANDREW C. MCCARTHY

former Chief Assistant U.S. Attorney; Senior Fellow, National Review Institute; Contributing Editor, National Review

PATRICK POOLE

Consultant to the military and law enforcement on anti-terrorism issues

JOSEPH E. SCHMITZ

former Inspector General, Department of Defense

TOM TRENTO

Executive Director, Florida Security Council

J. MICHAEL WALLER

Annenberg Professor of International Communication, Institute of World Politics, and Vice President for Information Operations, Center for Security Policy

DIANA WEST

author and columnist

R. JAMES WOOLSEY

former Director of Central Intelligence

DAVID YERUSHALMI, ESQ.
General Counsel to the Center for Security Policy

FOREWORD

Ever since 9/11, it has been a central tenet of America's national security establishment that the threat of jihadist terrorism and the proper way of contending with that danger have nothing to do with Islam – except to the extent al Qaeda (or, more recently, the Islamic State) "perverts" or "hijacks" that religion.

But what if this characterization of the problem we continue to face fifteen years on is **simply and utterly wrong**? What if there actually is a **direct tie** between the totalitarian doctrine that the authorities of Islam call "sharia" and the jihad (or holy war) it demands of adherents, some of which is manifested as terrifying violence?

What if, in addition, jihadists engage in *pre*-violent – and, in some ways, far more insidious – efforts to accomplish the same goal: the supremacy of sharia worldwide under a caliph?

These questions were the focus of an intensive six-month study by a remarkable group of highly accomplished civilian and military national security professionals. Notable among its members were: former Director of Central Intelligence R. James Woolsey, former Director of the Defense Intelligence Agency Lieutenant General Harry "Ed" Soyster, former Deputy Under Secretary of Defense for Intelligence Lieutenant General William G. "Jerry" Boykin and former Assistant U.S. Attorney Andrew C. McCarthy.

Together, this group formed a "Team B," modeled after a similar initiative that supplied at a critical moment during the Cold War an independent assessment of Soviet intentions and capabilities. Ultimately, that "second opinion," which debunked the official (Team A) orthodoxy about the USSR, helped inform and guide Mr. Reagan's opposition to the form of appeasement known at the time as "détente," and shaped his strategy as president to take down the USSR.

Like its predecessor, today's Team B II differs dramatically from the official U.S. government ("Team A") party line on the most important challenge of

our time. Entitled, **Sharia: The Threat to America**, the group's report counters the notion that the present totalitarian ideology bent on our destruction can be safely ignored, misconstrued or appeased in the name of the contemporary counterpart to détente: "engagement."

First published in December 2010, **Sharia: The Threat** documents a profoundly troubling reality. The Obama administration and its immediate predecessors *under both political parties*, along with many state and local governments, have been blind – in some cases willfully and in every case perilously so – to the harsh truth about: the nature of the enemy we confront; what actually animates him; the progress he is making towards achieving our destruction; and what we need to do to prevent his success.

This situation is dangerous in the extreme to our Constitution, freedoms, form of government and security. It must not be allowed to persist.

The Team B II report has made a vital contribution to the urgently needed national debate about the true wellspring of terrorism and the other manifestations of Islamic supremacism: sharia. The findings of this study are as compelling as they are authoritative.

This volume offers an abridged version of *Sharia: The Threat to America* featuring just its Executive Summary, Key Findings and Key Tenets of Sharia, thereby making accessible to the casual reader the most important concepts and findings of the original volume. We hope this introductory material will, however, spur your interest in digging deeper into the subject by reading the Team B II report in its entirety.

The unabridged version of *Sharia: The Threat to America* is available in paperback and Kindle versions on amazon.com. It may also be downloaded at no charge at www.SecureFreedom.org.

                    Frank J. Gaffney

                    President, Center for Security Policy

EXECUTIVE SUMMARY

Sun Tzu stressed the imperative of warriors understanding both themselves and their enemy: "If you know the enemy and know yourself, you need not fear the results of a hundred battles." The U.S. military has carefully followed Sun Tzu's guidance in the training and education of its warriors.

Yet, today, America is engaged in existential conflict with foes that have succeeded brilliantly in concealing their true identity and very dangerous capabilities. In this, they have been helped by our own willful blindness – a practice in which, given the real, present and growing danger, we simply can no longer afford to indulge. This report is a contribution toward knowing the enemy.

THE THREAT IS SHARIA

The enemy adheres to an all-encompassing Islamic political-military-legal doctrine known as sharia. Sharia obliges them to engage in jihad to achieve the triumph of Islam worldwide through the establishment of a global Islamic State governed exclusively by sharia, under a restored caliphate.

The good news is that millions of Muslims around the world – including many in America – do not follow the directives of sharia, let alone engage in jihad. The bad news is that this reality reflects the fact that the imposition of strict sharia doctrine is at different stages across Muslim-majority and -minority countries.

The appearance is thus created that there is variation in sharia. Of late, representatives of Muslim- and Arab-American groups[8] and their apologists[9] have been claiming that there is no single sharia, that it is subject to interpretation and no one interpretation is any more legitimate than any other.

In fact, for especially the Sunni and with regard to non-Muslims, there is ultimately but one sharia. It is totalitarian in character, incompatible with our Constitution and a threat to freedom here and around the world. Sharia's adherents are making a determined, sustained, and well-financed effort to impose it on all Muslims and non-Muslims, alike.

That effort is abetted enormously by several factors. Too many Muslims, to borrow a metaphor from Mao, provide the sea in which the jihadis swim. By offering little meaningful opposition to the jihadist agenda and by meekly submitting to it, a large number of Muslim communities and nations generally project a tacit agreement with jihadis' ends, if not with their means. At the very least, they exhibit an unwillingness to face the consequences of standing up to sharia's enforcers within Islam. Such consequences include the distinct possibility of being denounced as an apostate, a capital offense under sharia.

There are, moreover, Muslims around the world – including some in Europe, Canada, Australia and the United States – who *do* support sharia by various means. These include: (1) by contributing to "charity" (*zakat*), even though, according to sharia, those engaged in jihad are among the authorized recipient categories for what amounts to a mandatory tax;[10] (2) by inculcating their children with sharia at mosques or *madrassas*; and (3) by participating in, or simply failing to report, abhorrent behavior condoned or commanded by sharia (e.g., underage and forced marriage,[11] honor killing,[12] female genital mutilation,[13] polygamy,[14] and domestic abuse,[15] including marital rape[16]).

Evidence of the extent to which sharia is being insinuated into the fabric of American society abounds, if one is willing to see it. A particularly egregious example was the 2009 case of a Muslim woman whose request for a restraining order against her Moroccan husband who had serially tortured and raped her was denied by New Jersey family court Judge Joseph Charles. The judge ruled on the grounds that the abusive husband had acted according to his Muslim (sharia) beliefs, and thus not with criminal intent.

In this instance, a New Jersey appellate court overturned the ruling in July 2010, making clear that in the United States, the laws of the land derive from the Constitution and the alien dictates of sharia have no place in a U.S. courtroom.[17] Still, the fact that such a reversal was necessary is instructive.

MISPERCEIVING THE THREAT

Few Americans are aware of the diversity and success to date of such efforts to insinuate sharia into the United States – let alone the full implications of the mortal threat this totalitarian doctrine represents to our freedoms, society and government. Fewer still understand the nature of the jihad being waged to impose it here.

To be sure, since 9/11, most in this country have come to appreciate that America is put at risk by violent jihadis who launch military assaults and plot destructive attacks against our friends and allies, our armed forces and our homeland. Far less recognizable, however, is the menace posed by jihadist enemies who operate by deceit and stealth from inside the gates. The latter threat is, arguably, a far more serious one to open, tolerant societies like ours. This report is substantially devoted to laying bare the danger posed by so-called "non-violent" jihadists, exposing their organizational infrastructure and modus operandi and recommending actions that must be taken to prevent their success.

The first thing to understand about the jihadis who operate by stealth is that they have precisely the same dual objectives as the openly violent jihadists (including al Qaeda, Hezbollah, Hamas and the Taliban): global imposition of sharia and re-establishment of the Islamic caliphate to rule in accordance with it. They differ only with respect to timing and tactics. In fact, the seemingly innocuous outreach tactics of *dawa* are merely part of the initial stages of what the U.S. military would call "intelligence preparation of the battlefield" that is calculated favorably to sculpt the terrain over the long term, preceding the ultimate, violent seizure of the U.S. government and replacement of the U.S. Constitution with sharia.[18]

U.S. national security leaders, academia, the media and society as a whole have been rendered all but incapable of recognizing this dimension as part of the enemy jihad. A number of factors have contributed to that lack of situational awareness. For one, it follows decades during which pride in American heritage, traditions and values steadily has eroded and pro-sharia sheikhs have poured millions into U.S. Middle East studies and inter-religious dialogue programs.

At the same time, a massive propaganda operation has targeted Western society. Its immediate goal is to obscure the fact that jihadist violence and more stealthy supremacism is rooted in the Islamic texts, teachings, and interpretations that constitute sharia.

The net result of these combined forces is that the United States has been infiltrated and deeply influenced by an enemy within that is openly determined to replace the U.S. Constitution with sharia.

THE MUSLIM BROTHERHOOD

The most important entity promoting Islamic supremacism, sharia, and the caliphate through – at least for the moment – non-violent means is the Muslim Brotherhood (MB, or in Arabic, the Ikhwan). The MB defined this form of warfare as "civilization jihad" in its strategic document for North America, entitled the *Explanatory Memorandum: On the General Strategic Goal for the Group,* which was entered into evidence in the 2008 *United States v. Holy Land Foundation* trial.[19]

Written in 1991 by Mohamed Akram, a senior Hamas leader in the United States and a member of the Board of Directors of the Muslim Brotherhood in North America, the *Explanatory Memorandum* declared that the Islamic Movement is an MB effort led by the Ikhwan in America.[20] It went on to explain that the "Movement" is a "settlement" process to establish itself inside the United States and, once rooted, to undertake a "grand jihad" characterized as a "civilization jihadist" mission that is likewise led by the Muslim Brotherhood.[21]

Specifically, the document explained that the civilization jihadist process involves a "grand jihad in eliminating and destroying the Western civilization from within and 'sabotaging' its miserable house by their hands and the hands of the believers so that it is eliminated…."[22] Author Robert Spencer has popularized the term "stealth jihad"[23] to describe this part of the sharia adherents' civilization jihad. The two terms are used interchangeably in this report.

This commitment to employ whatever tactics are most expedient was expressed in 1966 by one of the Brotherhood's seminal ideologues, Sayyid Qutb, in his influential book, *Milestones*: "Wherever an Islamic community exists which is a concrete example of the Divinely-ordained system of life, it has a God-given right to step forward and take control of the political authority....When Allah restrained Muslims from jihad for a certain period, it was a question of strategy rather than of principle...:"[24]

Other, more contemporary affirmations of the Brotherhood's commitment to stealth jihad can be found in the words of some of the Ikhwan's most prominent operatives in America today. For example, Louay Safi, a leader of two Brotherhood fronts – the International Institute of Islamic Thought (IIIT) and the Islamic Society of North America (ISNA), has declared that, "The principle of jihad obligates the Muslims to maintain and achieve these objectives [i.e., the triumph of Islam and the institution of the caliphate]. The best way to achieve these objectives and most appropriate method upholding the principle of jihad is, however, a question of leadership and strategy." [25]

A particularly telling indication of the stealth jihad agenda comes from Omar Ahmad, one of the founders of the Brotherhood's Council on American Islamic Relations (CAIR) and an unindicted co-conspirator in the Holy Land Foundation trial for funding international terrorism from the United States.[26] Ahmad made a reference to the MB's dual-messaging, a form of esoteric communication in which words seem innocuous to the uninitiated, but which have definite meaning to those duly indoctrinated: "I believe that our problem is that we stopped working underground. We will recognize the source of any message which comes out of us. I mean, if a message is publicized, we will know... the media person among us will recognize that you send two messages: one to the Americans and one to the Muslims."[27]

Note the Muslim Brotherhood operative's differentiation between "Americans" and "Muslims," as if presuming that Muslims are not or should not be good Americans. This differentiation is clear in CAIR's own name. In short, it is the enemy among us, working out in the open but disguised by deceit, that poses the greater long-term threat to our legal system and way of life.

As this report demonstrates, many of the most prominent Muslim organizations in America are front groups for, or derivatives of, the Muslim Brotherhood.[28] New Brotherhood entities are added each year. That so hostile an entity enjoys such a large footprint and dominant position within our society speaks volumes about the Ikhwan's organizational and financial reach.²⁹ No other *Muslim* group in the United States has been able even remotely to rival the Ikhwan's resource base, organizational skill or financial resources.

Multiculturalism, political correctness, misguided notions of tolerance and sheer willful blindness have combined to create an atmosphere of confusion and denial in America about the current threat confronting the nation. Of particular concern is the fact that political and military leaders in the United States find it difficult and/or distasteful to explain the true nature of the enemy to the public, and even to discuss it among themselves. Even when presented with detailed factual briefings and voluminous information about the essential linkage between sharia and violent acts of terrorism, most simply refuse to speak candidly about that connection.

To the contrary, U.S. national intelligence, law enforcement and security leadership seems determined to hide the Islamic origins of jihadist terrorism from the public. Through internal policy as well as public statements, U.S. officials have devised and seek to impose purposefully obscure and counterfactual language, evidently selected to divert American attention away from the Arab/Muslim origins of sharia and the Islamic doctrine of jihad.³⁰

Particularly worrying is the fact that, as counterterrorism expert Patrick Poole has put it: "Senior Pentagon commanders have labored to define the threat out of existence."³¹ Despite the rapidly expanding incidence of jihadist attacks and plots inside this country – whose perpetrators readily explain their Muslim identity and motivation – officials persist doggedly (and implausibly) in insisting on "lone wolf," "homegrown radical," or "isolated extremist" descriptions of our foes. The most recent example of this phenomenon was the Pentagon's final after-action report on the Fort Hood massacre of November, 2009.³²

Why would those sworn to support and defend the Constitution behave in a manner so detrimental to national security? Perhaps it is out of fear and perhaps out of recognition that they have abdicated their professional duty to develop an appropriate national security response. Perhaps, as Poole says, "Pretending that the threat is random and unknowable gives them license to do nothing."³³ Ikhwan pushback and allegations of racism and bigotry make it professionally difficult to challenge the Muslim Brotherhood's propaganda and operations.

THE WELLSPRING OF JIHAD

The truth is that today's enemy is completely comprehensible and can be professionally analyzed and factually understood in precise and specific detail. When analysis is so conducted, it is clear that conformance to sharia in America constitutes as great a threat as any enemy the nation has ever confronted.

The Obama administration has nonetheless built upon the willful blindness-induced failures of previous administrations with respect to sharia. The incumbent president and his team have not only declared that there is no "War on Terror" for the United States. They insist – *reductio ad absurdum* and in conformance with the policy dictates of the Organization of the Islamic Conference (OIC), the second-largest multinational entity (after the United Nations) made up of 56 predominantly Muslim nations and the Palestine Authority – that Islam has nothing to do with terrorism. Such a statement can only be made because, as will be shown below, the OIC and others who adhere to and promote sharia do not define acts of jihad as "terrorism."

The U.S. government line remains unchanged even as our enemies make plain the connection between their aggressive behavior and sharia-adherent jihad. To cite but one example, Iran's President Mahmoud Ahmadinejad publicly describes the ongoing "historic war between the oppressor and the world of Islam."³⁴ Yet, Obama's top counterterrorism advisor, John Brennan, insists that the President does not accept that there is a "global war" with Islamic terrorists.

Brennan further announced that the term "jihadists" will no longer be used to describe our enemies. According to Mr. Brennan, to use the term "jihadists" in describing Islamic terrorists is a mistake because it is "a legitimate term, 'jihad' meaning to purify oneself or to wage a holy struggle for a moral goal." He maintains that this use of the term to describe al Qaeda's ruthless operatives "risks giving these murderers the religious legitimacy they desperately seek, but in no way deserve."³⁵ The problem with this formulation is that jihad as a "holy struggle for a moral goal" may not be in conflict with al Qaeda's "ruthless" operations.

At a speech in late May 2010 at the Center for Strategic and International Studies (CSIS), Brennan expanded on the theme: "Nor do we describe our enemy as 'jihadists' or 'Islamists' because jihad is a holy struggle, a legitimate tenet of Islam, meaning to purify oneself or one's community, and there is nothing holy or legitimate or Islamic about murdering innocent men, women and children."[36] Left unresolved by Brennan is whether sharia classifies non-Muslims as innocent.

A NEEDED REALITY CHECK

Brennan's statements reflect a common lack of understanding of the fundamentals of sharia, including the doctrinal basis of the Quran, *hadiths*, the role of abrogation, and that status of consensus in which sharia is rooted. In fact, Brennan's assertions directly contradict the teachings of leading Islamic scholars.

For example, even a cursory review of the writings of Islamic authorities shows that "jihad" is warfare against non-Muslims.[37] The top counterterrorism adviser to the President of the United States has a professional responsibility to know these facts.

Brennan is correct in one respect: America is not in a "war on terror." Terrorism is indeed merely a tactic, like aerial or naval bombardment, ambush, maneuver and other similar activities. But America is at war with a determined enemy who has yet to be honestly identified by anyone in a position of authority in the United States.

It is also accurate to label jihad as a "legitimate tenet of Islam." But neither sharia nor its practitioners, our enemy, define it in terms that are even close to what Brennan used at CSIS. The sharia definition of jihad and that of the jihadis are the same.

This is not a partisan critique of behavior uniquely exhibited by the incumbent administration, or by Democrats alone. For example, President George W. Bush noted on September 20, 2001 that "terrorists are traitors to their own faith" that "hijacked their own religion."[38] Regrettably, this and similar statements subsequently issued by various Bush administration officials set the stage for the misleading comments being uttered by their successors today.

Notably, these include President Obama's statement made on January 7, 2010, that, "We are at war; we are at war with al Qaeda."[39] The President was discussing the results of an investigation into the attempted Christmas Day bombing of a Northwest Airlines flight over Detroit by a young Muslim from Nigeria named Umar Farouk Abdulmutallab. Even some of the President's critics expressed relief that the Chief Executive was finally recognizing that the nation was indeed facing a genuine enemy (albeit one comprised of many elements besides al Qaeda).

Since sharia emerged as a real threat, Obama, like Brennan and most of the U.S. national security leadership, has failed to define or explain accurately the nature of an enemy that explicitly threatens the American way of life; indeed, this threat imperils the constitutional framework that drives the exceptionalism that way of life sustains.

In fact, the forces of sharia have been at war with non-Muslims for 1,400 years and with the United States of America for 200 years.[40] While the most recent campaign to impose this totalitarian code began in the late 20th Century, it is but the latest in a historical record of offensive warfare that stretches back to the origins of Islam itself.

When Army Major Nidal Hasan murdered thirteen people at Fort Hood, Texas on November 5, 2009, the media, as well as the FBI, searched for answers as to why this American-born military officer would commit such an unconscionable act – the worst terrorist attack on U.S. soil since September 11, 2001. While myriad theories and opinions were offered, few in the Administration, the media, academia or the rest of the elite seemed capable of comprehending the killer's motives – even as he expressly stated them for years leading up to the event.

In fact, Hasan fully articulated his intentions to senior officers in the U.S. Army Medical Corps years before his rampage, and the warnings were ignored when brought to higher ranks. In a fifty-slide briefing given to his medical school class in 2007, entitled "Koranic View as it Relates to Muslims in the U.S Military,"[41] Hasan explained the requirement that Muslims under Islamic law conduct jihad against non-Muslims, and he specifically defined the parameters within which Muslims must act. For

Hasan, the relevant parameter was being deployed to the Middle East as this would put him in a status where he could be required to "kill without right." As can be demonstrated in detail, Hasan's presentation tracks exactly with Islamic law[42] – and he should know since, at the time of the massacre, he was the acting imam for Fort Hood.

Had anyone in the audience been taught the enemy threat doctrine (i.e., sharia on jihad), Hasan's amazingly candid presentation, which thoroughly explained his concerns given the fundamental concepts of sharia, would have alerted authorities in time to prevent his attack. Furthermore, the briefing contained an explicit declaration of Hasan's allegiance as a Muslim soldier in the Army of Allah. And yet, seemingly, none of the audience of senior medical officers recognized the threat that Hasan posed to his fellow soldiers. Hasan announced himself an enemy combatant and no one was either able or willing to process that information properly.

THE ENEMY WITHIN

Instinctively, even Americans who are unfamiliar with the term "sharia" understand that it poses a threat. For example, focus groups have shown that, when asked about "the law of Saudi Arabia," there is a considerable awareness about its brutal repression of those subjected to it and its aggressive designs on the rest of humanity.

Most of the public believes that it is the terrorists who seek to advance sharia via violence who pose the greatest threat. While this may be an understandable conclusion, it also points to how uninformed the public actually is.

Our intelligence community and law enforcement entities have disrupted roughly thirty terrorist attacks since September 11, 2001, and demonstrated laudable vigilance in pursuit of terrorists. Still, the community's failures – Major Hasan; the Christmas Day bomber, Umar Farouk Abdulmutallab; and the Times Square bomber, Faisal Shahzad – highlight serious flaws that remain in our intelligence collection and understanding of the true nature of the threat we face. In the Christmas Day case, U.S. intelligence failed to act even when warned specifically in advance by Abdulmutallab's own father.

Yet, al Qaeda and other Islamist groups who perpetrate terrorist acts are *not* the most dangerous threat. These threats, regardless of their brutality, cannot bring America to submit to sharia – at least were they to act alone. While the terrorists can and will inflict great pain on the nation, the ultimate goal of sharia-adherent Islam cannot be achieved by these groups solely through acts of terrorism, without a more subtle, well-organized component operating in tandem with them.

That component takes the form of "civilization jihad." This form of warfare includes multi-layered cultural subversion, the co-opting of senior leaders, influence operations and propaganda and other means of insinuating sharia into Western societies. These are the sorts of techniques alluded to by Yusuf al-Qaradawi, the spiritual leader of the Muslim Brotherhood, when he told a Toledo, Ohio Muslim Arab Youth Association convention in 1995: 'We will conquer Europe, we will conquer America! Not through the sword, but through *dawa*."[43]

The prime practitioners of this stealthy form of jihad are the ostensibly "non-violent" Muslim Brothers and their front groups and affiliates. It must always be kept in mind that such tactics are "non-violent" not because the Brotherhood eschews violence out of principle, but rather because it has decided that this phase of battlefield preparation is better accomplished through stealthy means. The violence is always implicit in the overall strategy, albeit held in reserve for the final stages of the offensive. It is the combined effect of the violent and pre-violent strains of jihad that constitutes the most serious threat to America and its free people.

As the pages that follow document in detail, the Muslim Brotherhood has been in this country for decades and is an existential threat to American society and the fundamental liberties ordained and established by the Founding Fathers in the U.S. Constitution. Its own mission statement asserts that "the Ikhwan must understand that their work in America is a kind of grand Jihad in eliminating and destroying the Western civilization from within and 'sabotaging' its miserable house by their hands and the hands of the believers so that it is eliminated and God's religion is made victorious over all other religions."[44]

This carefully articulated mission flows ineluctably from sharia, which holds that only Allah can make laws and that democratic rule whereby people legislate is impermissible. Therefore, the destruction of Western-style governments and subjugation of free societies to the Ikhwan's view of Allah's will is obligatory for the Muslim Brotherhood, as for other adherents to sharia. Since America is the world's preeminent exponent of individual liberties and the most powerful democratic country, those who are fighting to establish the Islamic caliphate have targeted this nation for destruction – not necessarily in the military or physical sense of the word, but in the destruction of American society as we know it.

Ultimately, the Muslim Brotherhood intends for America to live under sharia. This ambition was explicitly stated in 1996 by Abdurahman Alamoudi, at the time one of the top agents of the Muslim Brotherhood operation in the United States. Back then, Alamoudi enjoyed access to the Clinton White House since, as the founder of the American Muslim Council and a director of numerous other Brotherhood fronts, he was considered a leading spokesman for the Muslim community in America. (He is currently serving a twenty-three year federal prison term on terrorism-related charges.)

At the Islamic Association of Palestine's annual convention in Illinois in 1996, Alamoudi declared: "I have no doubt in my mind, Muslims sooner or later will be the moral leadership of America. It depends on me and you, either we do it now or we do it after a hundred years, but this country will become a Muslim country."[45]

THE TACIT SUPPORTERS OF CIVILIZATION JIHAD

The Team B II Report details the Muslim Brotherhood's multi-phased plan of operations for the destruction of Western civilization. The successful execution of this plan depends on at least tacit support or submission from the Muslim population at large.

At the very least, popular Muslim passivity signals an unwillingness to face the consequences of standing up to the Muslim Brothers and other enforcers within Islam. Those consequences can be quite severe, starting with social ostracism and sometimes ending with death. Since the Ikhwan's instrument of discipline and control over their fellow Muslims is the fact that any criticism of sharia or the Quran can be considered to be apostasy, for which the penalty is death, enforcement through social pressure is simple and unseen. This is particularly true among Muslim immigrant communities that have fled such brutality in their native countries and come to America for shelter, only to find the threat emerge in their new homeland.

There are, moreover, Muslims in Europe and the United States who *do* support sharia by various means. As we have seen, these include mandatory *zakat* contributions to certain "charities" even when the "donor" knows that, under sharia, jihad is one of the authorized recipient categories[46]; indoctrinating children with sharia at mosques and madrassas; and by participating in or failing to report abhorrent behavior including child abuse[47], wife abuse[48], female genital mutilation[49], polygamy[50], underage[51] and forced marriage[52], marital rape[53] and "honor killing."[54] One appalling example offers an insight into the extent to which sharia is being insinuated into the fabric of American society: The 2009 case of a Muslim woman whose request for a legal restraining order against her Moroccan husband who had serially abused and raped her was denied by New Jersey family court Judge Joseph Charles. The judge ruled that the abusive husband had acted according to his Muslim (sharia) beliefs[55] and thus not with criminal intent.

Fortunately, a New Jersey appellate court overturned the ruling in July 2010, making clear that in the United States, the laws of the land derive from the Constitution and the alien dictates of sharia have no place in a U.S. courtroom.[56] Still, the fact that such a reversal was necessary is frighteningly instructive.

According to sharia, the Quran and *hadiths* (accounts of the actions and sayings of Mohammed) comprise the authoritative roadmap for Muslims and, hence, the Muslim Brotherhood. In accordance with that roadmap, its members – like other adherents to sharia[57] – are engaged in a global war of conquest.[58] One can see this battle campaign being executed in every part of the world. Europe is in a tremendous struggle with an ever-increasing and influential Islamic threat. Many Europeans are perplexed by what they see happening in their countries as Islam infiltrates every sector of their society. Notably, after the London subway bombing in 2005, many in the United Kingdom were astonished that British-born

Muslims identified first and foremost with Pakistan and sharia, rather than with the nation where they were born and raised and its traditional values.

Like most Americans, these Britons fail to understand that the sharia-adherent Muslims do not identify with any sovereign nation. They see themselves as Muslims first and part of the future caliphate. Nowhere has this world view been more clearly enunciated than in the words of the late Ayatollah Ruhollah Khomeini, spoken in 1980 about the country of his birth: "We do not worship Iran, we worship Allah....I say, let this land [Iran] burn. I say let this land go up in smoke, provided Islam emerges triumphant...."[59]

THE NEED FOR CORRECTIVE ACTION

Given the gravity of this threat, it is simply astounding that the United States has, to date, neither developed nor adopted a strategy for defeating sharia's designs, and the Muslim Brotherhood's efforts to realize them. This information is not even being taught at a basic level to FBI counterterrorism agents and analysts, nor is it taught at the Justice Department, Department of Homeland Security, the State or Defense Departments, or the CIA.

Amidst the increasingly heated assertion of First Amendment protections for the practice and promotion of sharia in America, almost entirely missing is any recognition of the fundamental incompatibility with Article VI's requirement that "this Constitution shall be...the supreme law of the land" inherent in efforts to insinuate Islamic law into the United States.

Such a deplorable state of affairs helps explain why there is no strategy to defeat the sharia movement: that movement and its agenda are simply not understood within the ranks of the organizations legally charged with protecting America and its Constitution from such threats.

It bears repeating: no such strategy can be put into place, let alone be successfully executed, as long as our national leadership refuses to define the enemy in realistic and comprehensive terms. If such ignorance is allowed to persist, the Muslim Brotherhood will continue infiltrating American society at every level and executing a very deliberate plan to manipulate the nation into piecemeal submission to sharia.

To discount the possibility that such a seemingly preposterous state of affairs will eventuate in America would be a serious mistake. It is one that many Europeans have been making for years. Experts like Bernard Lewis, the internationally acclaimed authority on Islam, are now saying that Europe will be an Islamic continent by the end of this century,[60] if not before. While the proportion of Muslims to non-Muslims in the United States is much smaller than in Europe, America's accelerating submission to sharia documented in the following pages suggests that this country, too, is at risk of being fundamentally and unacceptably altered.

Heretofore, the United States has confronted primarily external threats. Today, we are facing an internal threat that has masked itself as a religion and that uses the tolerance for religious practice guaranteed by the Constitution's First Amendment to parry efforts to restrict or prevent what amount to seditious activities. In the process, the First Amendment itself is being infringed upon, as Muslim Brothers and others demand that free speech be barred where it gives offense to them – effectively imposing sharia blasphemy laws in this country.

For these reasons, among others, it should be understood that sharia is fundamentally about power, namely the enforcement of a body of law, not faith. In the words of the Muslim Brotherhood's Sayyid Qutb: "Whenever an Islamic community exists which is a concrete example of the Divinely-ordained system of life, it has a God-given right to step forward and control the political authority so that it may establish the divine system on earth, while it leaves the matter of belief to individual conscience."[61]

Sharia dictates a comprehensive and totalitarian system of laws, an aggressive military doctrine, an all-encompassing socio-economic program and a ruthless enforcement mechanism. It is, in short, a complete way of life. It is against this backdrop that the obligation sharia demands of its followers – namely, to conduct a global campaign to replace non-Muslim governments with Islamic States governed by Islamic law, to conquer *Dar al-Harb* (the House of War) for *Dar al-Islam* (the House of Islam) – must be seen as an illegal effort to supplant our Constitution with another legal code, not a religious practice protected by that document. Islamic scholar Majid Khadduri put it this way:

"It follows that the existence of a *Dar al-Harb* is ultimately outlawed under the Islamic jural order; that the dar al-Islam is permanently under jihad obligation until the *Dar al-Harb* is reduced to nonexistence; and that any community accepting certain disabilities – must submit to Islamic rule and reside in the dar al-Islam or be bound as clients to the Muslim community. The universalism of Islam, in its all-embracing creed, is imposed on the believers as a continuous process of warfare, psychological and political if not strictly military."[62]

Yet, many in this country – particularly in governmental, academic, and media elites – have shown themselves susceptible to the Muslim Brotherhood's strategy for waging sabotage against the United States in order to destroy "its miserable house...by their own hand." They are enabling sharia's spread by enforcing a tolerance of that doctrine under the rubric of freedom of religion and diversity, instead of recognizing it for the seditious and anti-constitutional agenda it openly espouses.

In the words of Muslim scholar Shamim Siddiqi: "The movement may also seek legal protection from the court for fundamental human rights *to propagate what its adherents believe to be correct* and to profess the same through democratic, peaceful and constitutional means."[63] (Emphasis added.)

Recent research indicates that in many mosques across the country the overthrow of the U.S. Constitution is being encouraged in the printed material offered on-site or in the textbooks used in children's classes, if not directly from the Friday pulpit.[64]

In addition, the 2008 Holy Land Foundation trial in Dallas, Texas, provided evidence that the majority of Islamic organizations in America are affiliates of or associated with the Muslim Brotherhood in some way and many of them are raising funds for jihad.[65] The convictions of all defendants in that case make clear that such behavior is not protected by the First Amendment. And yet, American elites still deal with sharia as just a religious system, when in fact it is as totalitarian a political program as ever were those of communism, fascism, National Socialism, or Japanese imperialism.

Military historians and combat veterans understand that it is far easier to defend against an attack that comes from an enemy outside one's defensive perimeter. In that case, the defending army need only train its fire outwards and have no fear of fratricide. By contrast, the most difficult attack to defend against is the one that comes from *inside* the defensive perimeter, because distinguishing the enemy from friendly forces is problematic.

That is the situation in America today. *We have an enemy inside our perimeter.* But for this nation, the challenge is not just an inability to distinguish friend from foe. Rather, it is an unwillingness to do so.

As the succeeding pages establish in greater detail, accurate and highly relevant information is available concerning what the Muslim Brotherhood and other sharia-adherent Muslims are doing in America, their goals and strategy. Much of that information comes from the Brotherhood's own documents and leadership statements.

Other insights can be obtained from those who were at one time part of the Muslim Brotherhood, but have chosen a new direction for their lives. Three such individuals – Walid Shoebat (formerly with the Palestinian Liberation Organization or PLO),[66] Kamal Saleem (former Muslim Brotherhood),[67] and Mosab Yousef (former Hamas and author of *Son of Hamas*)[68] – are proclaiming to all who will hear them that the Muslim Brotherhood is in America to destroy our Constitution and replace it with sharia. These brave men are helping to define the enemy. Their testimony, taken together with that available from other sources, leaves us with no excuse for remaining ignorant of the truth.

Armed with that truth – as compiled and analyzed in the Team B II report – the American people and their leaders are in a position to comprehend fully the nature of the threat posed by sharia and by those who seek through violence or stealthy subversion to impose it upon us. This knowledge obligates one to take action.

RECOMMENDATIONS

While detailed recommendations for adopting a more prudential and effective strategy for surviving sharia's onslaught are beyond the scope of this study, several policy and programmatic changes are in order. These include:

- U.S. policymakers, financiers, businessmen, judges, journalists, community leaders and the public at large must be equipped with an accurate understanding of the nature of sharia and the necessity of keeping America sharia-free. At a minimum, this will entail resisting – rather than acquiescing to – the concerted efforts now being made to allow that alien legal code to become established in this country as an alternate, parallel system to the Constitution and the laws enacted pursuant to it. Arguably, this is already in effect for those who have taken an oath to "support and defend" the Constitution, because the requirement is subsumed in that oath.

- U.S. government agencies and organizations should cease their outreach to Muslim communities through Muslim Brotherhood fronts whose mission is to destroy our country from within, as such practices are both reckless and counterproductive. Indeed, these activities serve to legitimate, protect and expand the influence of our enemies. They conduce to no successful legal outcome that cannot be better advanced via aggressive prosecution of terrorists, terror-funders and other lawbreakers. The practice also discourages patriotic Muslims from providing actual assistance to the U.S. government lest they be marked for ostracism or worse by the Ikhwan and other sharia-adherent members of their communities.

- In keeping with Article VI of the Constitution, extend bans currently in effect that bar members of hate groups such as the Ku Klux Klan, and endorsers of child abuse and other crimes, from holding positions of trust in federal, state, or local governments or the armed forces of the United States to those who espouse or support sharia. Instead, every effort should be made to identify and empower Muslims who are willing publicly to denounce sharia.

- Practices that promote sharia – notably, sharia-compliant finance and the establishment or promotion in public spaces or with public funds or facilities and activities that give preferential treatment to sharia's adherents – are incompatible with the Constitution and the freedoms it enshrines and must be proscribed.

- Sedition is prohibited by law in the United States. To the extent that imams and mosques are being used to advocate sharia in America, they are promoting seditious activity and should be warned that they will be subject to investigation and prosecution.

- Textbooks used in both secular educational systems and Islamic schools must not promote sharia, its tenets, or the notion that America must submit to its dictates. Schools that promote anti-constitutional teaching should be denied taxpayer funding and lose their charters, accreditation and charitable tax status.

- Compounds and communities that seek to segregate themselves on the basis of sharia law, apply it alongside or in lieu of the law of the land or otherwise establish themselves as "no-go" zones for law enforcement and other authorities must be thwarted in such efforts. In this connection, assertion of claims to territory around segregationist mosques should be proscribed.

- Immigration of those who adhere to sharia must be precluded, as was previously done with adherents to the seditious ideology of communism.

Such measures will, of course, be controversial in some quarters. They will certainly be contested by sharia-adherent Muslims committed to jihad and others who, in the name of exercising or protecting civil liberties, are enabling the destruction of those liberties in furtherance of sharia. Far from being dispositive, their opposition should be seen as an opportunity – a chance, at a minimum, for a long-overdue debate about the sorts of policies that have brought the West in general and the United States in particular to the present, parlous state of affairs. If this study catalyzes and usefully informs that debate, it will have succeeded.

KEY FINDINGS

- The United States is under attack by foes who are openly animated by what is known in Islam as sharia (Islamic law). According to sharia, every faithful Muslim is obligated to wage jihad, whether violent or not, against those who do not adhere to this comprehensive, totalitarian, political-military code. The enemy's explicit goal is to establish a global Islamic State, known as the caliphate, governed by sharia.

- Sharia is based on the Quran (held by all Muslims to be the "uncreated" word of Allah as dictated to Mohammed), *hadiths* (sayings of Mohammed) and agreed interpretations. It commands Muslims to carry out jihad (holy war) indefinitely until all of the *Dar al-Harb* (i.e., the House of War, where sharia is not enforced) is brought under the domination of *Dar al-Islam* (the House of Islam – or literally the House of Submission, where sharia *is* enforced).

- Sharia dictates that non-Muslims be given three choices: convert to Islam and conform to sharia; submit as second-class citizens (*dhimmis*); or be killed. Not all classes are given the second option.

- Both Islamic terrorism and pre-violent, "civilization jihad" (popularly referred to as "stealth jihad") are commanded by sharia. That is not only the view of "extremists" and "fringe" elements "hijacking the religion," but of many authorities of Islam widely recognized as mainstream and drawing upon orthodox texts, interpretations and practices of the faith.

- The Muslim Brotherhood is the font of modern Islamic jihad. It is dedicated to the same global supremacist objectives as those (like al Qaeda and the Taliban) who share its adherence to sharia but who believe that violent jihad is more likely to more quickly produce the common goal of a global caliphate.

- The Brotherhood's internal documents make clear that civilization jihad is subversion waged by stealth instead of violence only until such time as Muslims are powerful enough to progress to violent jihad for the final conquest.

- Those who work to insinuate sharia into the United States intend to subvert and replace the Constitution (itself a violation of Article VI) because, according to sharia, freedom of religion, other civil liberties enshrined in the Constitution, and the rule of man-made law are incompatible with Islam (which means "submission").

- The sharia-adherent enemy prioritizes information warfare, manifested in American society as propaganda, political warfare, psychological warfare, influence operations and subversion of our foundational institutions. Our government structure fails to recognize this strategy because it is focused so exclusively on kinetic attacks. As a result, the United States remains crippled in its inability to engage this enemy effectively *on his primary battlefield.*

- The Brotherhood exploits the atmosphere of intimidation created by Islamic terrorists, thus inculcating in the West a perceived need for "outreach" to the "Muslim community" which, in turn, opens up opportunities to pursue a campaign of stealthy infiltration into American and other Western societies. The combined effect of such "civilization jihad" and jihadism of the violent kind may prove to be considerably more dangerous for this country and other Western societies than violent jihad alone.

- The Brotherhood has succeeded in penetrating our educational, legal and political systems, as well as top levels of government, intelligence, the media, and U.S. military, virtually paralyzing our ability to plan or respond effectively.

- Muslim Brotherhood organizations conduct outreach to the government, law enforcement, media, religious community, and others for one reason: to *subvert* them in furtherance of their objective, which is implementation of Islamic law.

- An informed and determined counter-strategy to defend the Constitution from sharia can yet succeed – provided it is undertaken in the prompt, timely and comprehensive manner recommended by Team B II.

KEY TENETS OF SHARIA

The following are some of the most important – and, particularly for Western non-Muslims, deeply problematic – tenets of sharia, arranged in alphabetical order. The citations drawn from the Quran, schools of Islam and other recognized sources are offered as illustrative examples of the basis for such practices under sharia.

1. **Abrogation** (*'Al-mansukh wa al-nasikh'* in Arabic—the abrogated and the abrogating): verses that come later in the Quran, chronologically, supersede, or abrogate, the earlier ones. In effect, this results in the more moderate verses of the Meccan period being abrogated by the later, violent, Medinan verses. "When we cancel a message, or throw it into oblivion, we replace it with one better or one similar. Do you not know that Allah has power over all things?" (Quran 2:106)

2. **Adultery** (*'Zina'* in Arabic): unlawful intercourse is a capital crime under sharia, punishable by lashing and stoning to death. "Nor come nigh to adultery: for it is a shameful deed and an evil, opening the road to other evils." (Q 17:32) "The woman and the man guilty of adultery or fornication, flog each of them with a hundred stripes; let not compassion move you in their case, in a matter prescribed by Allah, if ye believe in Allah and the Last Day: and let a party of the Believers witness the punishment." (Q 24:2) "It is not lawful to shed the blood of a Muslim except for one of three sins: a married person committing fornication, and in just retribution for premeditated murder, and [for sin of treason involving] a person renouncing Islam, and thus leaving the community [to join the enemy camp in order to wage war against the faithful]." (Al-Bukhari, Muslim, Abu Dawud, Tirmidhi, and An-Nasa'i)

3. **Apostasy** (*'Irtidad'* or *'Ridda'* in Arabic): The established ruling of sharia is that apostates are to be killed wherever they may be

found. "Anyone who, after accepting Faith in Allah, utters Unbelief, except under compulsion, his heart remaining firm in Faith—but such as open their heart to Unbelief—on them is Wrath from Allah, and theirs will be a dreadful Penalty." (Q 16:106)

"Some atheists were brought to Ali and he burnt them. The news of this event, reached Ibn Abbas who said, 'If I had been in his place, I would not have burnt them, as Allah's messenger forbade it, saying, 'Do not punish anybody with Allah's punishment (fire).' I would have killed them according to the statement of Allah's Messenger, 'Whoever changed his Islamic religion, then kill him.'" (Bukhari, Volume 9, #17)

"Leaving Islam is the ugliest form of unbelief (*kufr*) and the worst......When a person who has reached puberty and is sane voluntarily apostasizes from Islam, he deserves to be killed...There is no indemnity for killing an apostate..." (*'Umdat al-Salik*, Reliance of the Traveler, Chapter o8.0-o8.4)

4. **Democracy & Islam:** Any system of man-made law is considered illicit under Islamic law, for whose adherents Allah already has provided the only law permitted, sharia. Islam and western-style democracy can never co-exist in harmony. "And if any fail to judge by the light of what Allah has revealed, they are no better than unbelievers." (Q 5:47) "Sovereignty in Islam is the prerogative of Almighty Allah alone. He is the absolute arbiter of values and it is His will that determines good and evil, right and wrong." (Mohammed Hashim Kamali, *Principles of Islamic Jurisprudence*, 3d rev. ed., (Cambridge, UK: The Islamic Text Society, 2003), 8.)

"The sharia cannot be amended to conform to changing human values and standards. Rather, it is the absolute norm to which all human values and conduct must conform." (Muslim Brotherhood spiritual leader Yousef al-Qaradawi)

5. **Female Genital Mutilation:** "Circumcision is obligatory....for both men and women." *('Umdat al-Salik,* e4.3)

6. **Gender Inequality:** Sharia explicitly relegates women to a status inferior to men.

    - Testimony of a woman before a judge is worth half that of a man: "And get two witnesses, not of your own men, and if there are not two men, then a man and two women, such as ye choose for witnesses." (Q 2:282)

    - Women are to receive just one half the inheritance of a male: "Allah thus directs you as regards your children's inheritance: to the male, a portion equal to that of two females...." (Q 4:11)

    - Muslim men are given permission by Allah in the Quran to beat their wives: "As to those women on whose part ye fear disloyalty and ill conduct, admonish them first, next refuse to share their beds, and last, beat them." (Q 4:34)

    - Muslim men are given permission by Allah to commit marital rape, as they please: "Your wives are as a tilth unto you, so approach your tilth when or how ye will...." (Q 2:223)

    - Muslim men are permitted to marry up to four wives and to keep concubines in any number: "...Marry women of your choice, two, or three, or four; but if ye fear that ye shall not be able to deal justly with them, then only one, or a captive that your right hands possess..." (Q 4:3)

    - Muslim women may marry only one Muslim man and are forbidden to marry a non-Muslim: "And give not (your daughters) in marriage to Al-Mushrikun [non-Muslims] till they believe in Allah alone and verily a believing slave is better than a (free) Mushrik, even though he pleases you...." (Q 2:221)

    - A woman may not travel outside the home without the permission of her male guardian and must be accompanied by a male family member if she does so: "A woman may not leave the city without her husband or a member of her unmarriageable kin....accompanying her, unless the journey is obligatory, like the hajj. It is unlawful for her to travel otherwise, and unlawful for her husband to allow her." (*'Umdat al-Salik*, m10.3)

- Under sharia, to bring a claim of rape, a Muslim woman must present four male Muslim witnesses in good standing. Islam thus places the burden of avoiding illicit sexual encounters entirely on the woman. In effect, under sharia, women who bring a claim of rape without being able to produce the requisite four male Muslim witnesses are admitting to having had illicit sex. If she or the man is married, this amounts to an admission of adultery. The following Quranic passages, while explicitly applying to men are cited by sharia authorities and judges in adjudicating rape cases: "And those who accuse free women then do not bring four witnesses (to adultery), flog them..." Q 24:4) "Why did they not bring four witnesses to prove it? When they have not brought the witnesses, such men, in the sight of Allah, stand forth themselves as liars!" (Q 24:13)

- A Muslim woman who divorces and remarries loses custody of children from a prior marriage: "A woman has no right to custody of her child from a previous marriage when she remarries because married life will occupy her with fulfilling the rights of her husband and prevent her from tending the child." (*'Umdat al-Salik*, m13.4)

7. **"Honor" Killing** (aka Muslim family executions): A Muslim parent faces no legal penalty under Islamic law for murdering his child or grandchild: "...not subject to retaliation" is "a father or mother (or their fathers or mothers) for killing their offspring, or offspring's offspring." (*'Umdat al-Salik*, o1.1-2)

8. **Hudud Punishments:** The plural of *hadd*, is "a fixed penalty prescribed as a right of Allah. Because *hudud* penalties belong to Allah, Islamic law does not permit them to be waived or commuted."[69]

    - "Let not compassion move you in their case, in a matter prescribed by Allah, if you believe in Allah and the Last Day: and let a party of believers witness their punishment." (Q 24:2)

    - "On that account, We ordained for the Children of Israel that if any one slew a [Muslim] person – unless it be for murder or for spreading mischief in the land – it would be as if he slew the whole people.... The punishment of those who wage war against Allah and his apostle, and strive with might and main for mischief through the land is execution, or crucifixion, or the cutting off of hands and feet from opposite sides, or exile from the land..." (Q 32-33)

    - From the *Kitab al-kaba'ir* (*Book of Enormities*) of Imam Dhahabi, who defines an *enormity* as any sin entailing either a threat of punishment in the hereafter explicitly mentioned by the Koran or hadith, a prescribed legal penalty (Hadd), or being accursed by Allah or His messenger (Allah bless him & give him peace). (*'Umdat al-Salik*, Book P "Enormities," at § p0.0)

    - "Sharia stipulates these punishments and methods of execution such as amputation, crucifixion, flogging, and stoning, for offenses such as adultery, homosexuality, killing without right, theft, and 'spreading mischief in the land' because these punishments were mandated by the Qur'an or Sunnah." (*Islamic Hudood Laws in Pakistan*, Edn 1996, 5.)

9. **Islamic Supremacism:** belief that Islam is superior to every other culture, faith, government, and society and that it is ordained by Allah to conquer and dominate them: "And whoever

desires a religion other than Islam, it shall not be accepted from him, and in the hereafter he shall be one of the losers." (Q 3:85):

- "Ye are the best of Peoples, evolved for mankind." (Q 3:110)
- Non-Muslims are "the most vile of created beings" (Q 98:6)
- Be "merciful to one another, but ruthless to the unbelievers" (Q 48:29)
- "It is the nature of Islam to dominate, not to be dominated, to impose its law on all nations and to extend its power to the entire planet." (Hassan al-Banna, founder of the Muslim Brotherhood)
- "Islam isn't in America to be equal to any other faith, but to become dominant. The Koran should be the highest authority in America, and Islam the only accepted religion on Earth." (Omar Ahmad, Council on American Islamic Relations co-founder/Board Chairman, 1998)

10. **Jew Hatred:** Antisemitism is intrinsic to sharia and is based on the genocidal behavior of Mohammed himself in wiping out the entire Jewish population of the Arabian Peninsula.

- "And certainly you have known those among you who exceeded the limits of the Sabbath, as we said to them: Be as apes, despised and hated." (Q 2:65)
- "And you will most certainly find them [the Jews] the greediest of men for life, greedier than even those who are polytheists..." (Q 2:96)
- "O you who believe! Do not take the Jews and the Christians for friends; for they are friends but of each other; and whoever amongst you takes them for a

friend, then surely he is one of them; surely Allah does not guide the unjust people." (Q 5:51)

- "Fight those who believe not in Allah nor the Last Day, nor hold that forbidden which hath been forbidden by Allah and his apostle, nor acknowledge the religion of truth, even if they be of the People of the Book [Christians and Jews], until they pay the *jizya* with willing submission and feel themselves subdued." (Q 9:29)

11. **Jihad:** Jihad is warfare to spread Islam:

- "Fight and kill the disbelievers wherever you find them, and seize them, beleaguer them and lie in wait for them in every stratagem of war..." (Q 9:5)
- "Fight those who believe not in Allah nor the Last Day, nor hold that forbidden by Allah and His Messenger, nor acknowledge the Religion of Truth, from among the People of the Book, until they pay the *jizya* with willing submission and feel themselves subdued." (Q 9:29)
- "So fight them until there is no more *fitna* and all submit to the religion of Allah alone." (Q 8:39)
- "I have been commanded to fight people until they testify that there is no god but Allah and that Mohammed is the Messenger of Allah, and perform the prayer, and pay the *zakat*. If they say it, they have saved their blood and possessions from me, except for the rights of Islam over them. And their final reckoning is with Allah" (Sahih Bukhari and Sahih Muslim – agreed upon – as cited in '*Umdat al-Salik* o9.1 Jihad)
- "Jihad means to wage war against non-Muslims and is etymologically derived from the word *mujahada*, signifying warfare to establish the religion." ('*Umdat al-Salik*, o9.0, Jihad)

- "Islam makes it incumbent on all adult males, provided they are not disabled or incapacitated, to prepare themselves for the conquest of [other] countries so that the writ of Islam is obeyed in every country in the world.... But those who study Islamic Holy War will understand why Islam wants to conquer the whole world.... Those who know nothing of Islam pretend that Islam counsels against war. Those [who say this] are witless. Islam says: Kill all the unbelievers just as they would kill you all!" (Ayatollah Khomeini as quoted by Amir Taheri.)

- "Does this mean that Muslims should sit back until they are devoured by [the unbelievers]? Islam says: Kill them [the non-Muslims], put them to the sword and scatter [their armies]. Does this mean sitting back until [non-Muslims] overcome us? Islam says: Kill in the service of Allah those who may want to kill you! Does this mean that we should surrender [to the enemy]? Islam says: Whatever good there is exists thanks to the sword and in the shadow of the sword! People cannot be made obedient except with the sword! The sword is the key to Paradise, which can be opened only for the Holy Warriors! There are hundreds of other [Quranic] psalms and *Hadiths* [sayings of the prophet] urging Muslims to value war and to fight. Does all this mean that Islam is a religion that prevents men from waging war? I spit upon those foolish souls who make such a claim." (Ayatollah Khomeini as quoted by Amir Taheri.[70])

12. **Lying/*Taqiyya*:** It is permissible for a Muslim to lie, especially to non-Muslims, to safeguard himself personally or to protect Islam.

    - "Let not the believers take the disbelievers as friends instead of the believers, and whoever does that, will never be helped by Allah in any way, *unless you indeed fear a danger from them. And Allah warns you against Himself, and to Allah is the final return."* (Q 3:28)

- *"'Unless you indeed fear a danger from them'* meaning, except those believers who in some areas or times fear for their safety from the disbelievers. In this case, such believers are allowed to show friendship to the disbelievers outwardly, but never inwardly.... 'We smile in the face of some people although our hearts curse them.'" (*Tafsir Ibn Kathir*, vol. 2, 141)

- "Mohammed said, 'War is deceit.'" (Bukhari vol. 4:267 and 269)

- "He who makes peace between the people by inventing good information or saying good things, is not a liar." (Bukhari vol. 3:857 p.533)

13. **Slander/Blasphemy:** In sharia, slander means anything that might offend a Muslim, even if it is true: "... The reality of talebearing lies in divulging a secret, in revealing something confidential whose disclosure is resented. A person should not speak of anything he notices about people besides that which benefits a Muslim to relate or prevent disobedience." (*'Umdat al-Salik*, r3.1)

14. **Underage Marriage:** Islamic doctrine permits the marriage of pre-pubescent girls. There is no minimum age for a marriage contract and consummation may take place when the girl is age eight or nine.

    - "And those of your women as have passed the age of monthly courses [periods], for them the *'Iddah* [prescribed period before divorce is final], if you have doubts (about their periods), is three months, *and for those who have no courses [(i.e. they are still immature)* their 'Iddah (prescribed period) is three months likewise, except in case of death]. And for those who are pregnant (whether they are divorced or their husbands are dead), their 'Iddah (prescribed period) is until they deliver (their burdens), and whosoever fears Allah and keeps his duty to Him, He will make his matter easy for him." (Q 65:4)

- "Aisha narrated: that the Prophet married her when she was six years old and he consummated his marriage when she was nine years old, and then she remained with him for nine years (i.e., till his death)." (*Sahih al-Bukhari*, vol. 7, Book 62, Number 64; see also Numbers 65 and 88)"They may not have menstruated as yet either because of young age, or delayed menstrual discharge as it happens in the case of some women, or because of no discharge at all throughout life which, though rare, may also be the case. In any case, the waiting-period of such a woman is the same as of the woman who has stopped menstruation, that is, three months from the time divorce was pronounced.

- "Here, one should bear in mind the fact that, according to the explanations given in the Qur'an, the question of the waiting period arises in respect of the women with whom marriage may have been consummated, for there is no waiting-period in case divorce is pronounced before the consummation of marriage. (Al-Ahzab: 49). Therefore, making mention of the waiting-period for girls who have not yet menstruated, clearly proves that it is not only permissible to give away the girl at this age but it is permissible for the husband to consummate marriage with her. Now, obviously no Muslim has the right to forbid a thing which the Qur'an has held as permissible." (Syed Abu-Ala' Maududi, *Towards Understanding the Qur'an*, volume 5, p. 620, note 13)

15. **Zakat**: the obligation for Muslims to pay *zakat* arises out of Quran Verse 9:60 and is one of the Five Pillars of Islam. *Zakat* may be given only to Muslims, never to non-Muslims.

- *Zakat* is for the poor and the needy, and those employed to administer the (funds); for those whose hearts have been (recently) reconciled (to Truth); for those in bondage and in debt; in the cause of Allah; and for the wayfarer: (thus is it) ordained by Allah, and Allah is full of knowledge and wisdom. (Q 9:60) "Of their goods take alms so that thou mightiest purify and sanctify them...." (Q 9:103) "Zakat is obligatory: (a) for every free Muslim and (b) who has possessed a *zakat-payable amount* [the minimum that necessitates *zakat*] (*'Umdat al-Salik*, h1.1)

- According to sharia, there are eight categories of recipients for *Zakat:* The poor; Those short of money; *Zakat* workers (those whose job it is to collect the *zakat*); Those whose hearts are to be reconciled; Those purchasing their freedom; Those in debt; Those fighting for Allah (Jihad); Travelers needing money (*'Umdat al-Salik*, h8.7-h8.18)

- "It is not permissible to give *Zakat* to a non-Muslim..." (*'Umdat al-Salik*, h8.24)

REFERENCES

8, for example, Congressional Muslim Staff Association briefing on Capitol Hill, September 1, 2010.

10 Ahmad ibn Naqib al-Misri, Umdat al-Salik (*Reliance of the Traveller: A Classic Manu See al of Islamic Law*), rev. ed., trans. Nuh Ha Mim Keller. (Beltsville, Amana Publications, 1994) ', Chapter h8.17, 272.

11 Quran Sura 65:4 describes the waiting period for a divorce to be final: "Such of your women as have passed the age of monthly courses, for them the prescribed period, if ye have any doubts, is three months; and for those who have no courses (it is the same)."

12 al-Misri, *Reliance of the Traveler*, Chapter ol.2, pgs. 583-84 enumerates those categories of Muslims who "are not subject to retaliation" for killing: "(4) a father or mother (or their fathers or mothers) for killing their offspring, or offspring's offspring."

13 al-Misri, *Reliance of the Traveler*, Chapter o4.3: "Circumcision is obligatory (for both men and women.....for women, removing the prepuce of the clitoris...)."

14 Quran Sura 4:3: "...marry women of your choice, two, or three, or four..."

15 Quran Sura 4:34: "....And to those women on whose part ye fear disloyalty and ill-conduct, admonish them (first), (next) refuse to share their beds, (and last) beat them...."

16 Quran Sura 2:233: "Your wives are as a tilth unto you, so approach your tilth when or how ye will...."

17 Maxim Lott, "Advocates of Anti-Sharia Measures Alarmed by Judge's Ruling," *Fox News*, August 5, 2010, accessed August 6, 2010, http://www.foxnews.com/us/2010/08/05/advocates-anti-sharia-measures-alarmed-judges-ruling/

18 Shamim A Siddiqi, *Methodology of Dawah Ilallah In American Perspective*, (Brooklyn, NY, 1989). The text in full is available online, accessed July 18, 2010, http://www.dawahinamericas.com/bookspdf/MethodologyofDawah.pdf

19 *Explanatory Memorandum*, 18.

20 Paragraph 1, §§ 1 and 2, *Explanatory Memorandum*, 18. Reads:

>One: The Memorandum is derived from:
>
>1 - The general strategic goal of the Group in America which was approved by the *Shura* Council and the Organizational Conference for the year [1987] is "Enablement of Islam in North America, meaning: establishing an effective and a stable *Islamic Movement led by the Muslim Brotherhood* which adopts Muslims' causes domestically and globally, and which works to expand the observant Muslim base, aims at unifying and directing Muslims' efforts, presents Islam as a civilization alternative, and supports the global Islamic State wherever it is."
>
>Two: An Introduction to the Explanatory Memorandum:
>In order to begin with the explanation, we must "summon" the following question and place it in front of our eyes as its relationship is important and necessary with the strategic goal and the explanation project we are embarking on. The question we are facing is: "How do you like to see the Islam Movement in North America in ten years?", or "taking along" the following sentence when planning and working, "Islamic Work in North America in the year (2000): A Strategic Vision". Also, we must summon and take along "elements" of the general strategic goal of the Group in North America and I will intentionally repeat them in numbers. They are:
>1- Establishing an effective and stable *Islamic Movement led by the Muslim Brotherhood*.

21 Paragraph 4, *Explanatory Memorandum*, 20. Reads:

>Four: The Process of Settlement:
>
>In order for Islam and its *Movement* to become "a part of the homeland" in which it lives, "stable" in its land, "rooted" in the spirits and minds of its people, "enabled" in the lives of its society and has firmly-established "organizations" on which the Islamic structure is built and with which the testimony of civilization is achieved, the *Movement* must plan and struggle to obtain "the keys" and the tools of this process in carry out this grand mission as a "*Civilization Jihadist*" responsibility which lies on the shoulders of Muslims and - on top of them - the *Muslim Brotherhood* in this country. Among these keys and tools are the following ...

22 Paragraph 4, § 4, *Explanatory Memorandum*, 21. Reads:

>4- Understanding the role of the Muslim Brother in North America:

> The process of settlement is a "Civilization-Jihadist Process" with all the word means. The *Ikhwan* must understand that their work in America is a kind of grand Jihad in eliminating and destroying the Western civilization from within and "sabotaging" its miserable house by their hands and the hands of the believers so that it is eliminated and God's religion is made victorious over all other religions. Without this level of understanding, we are not up to this challenge and have not prepared ourselves for Jihad yet. It is a Muslim's destiny to perform Jihad and work wherever he is and wherever he lands until the final hour comes, and there is no escape from that destiny except for those who chose to slack. But, would the slackers and the Mujahedeen be equal.

23 Robert Spencer, *Stealth Jihad: How Radical Islam is Subverting America Without Guns or Bombs*, Regnery Publishing, 2008.

24 Sayyid Qutb, *Milestones*, (Salimiah, Kuwait: International Islamic Federation of Student Organizations.1978 [written 1966]), 139.

25 Louay M. Safi, *Peace and the Limits of War: Transcending Classical Conception of Jihad.* (Herndon, VA: IIIT, 2001), 42.

26 U.S. v Holy Land Foundation case, No. 43, Attachment A, List of Unindicted Co-conspirators and/or Joint Ventures, United States of America vs. Holy Land Foundation, United States District Court for Northern District of Texas, Dallas Division, (Case 3:04-cr-00240, Document 656-2), 29 March 2007, at 8, at http://www.websupp.com/data/NDTX/3:04-cr-00240-635-NDTX.pdf or at http://www.nefafoundation.org/miscellaneous/HLF/US_v_HLF_Unindicted_Coconspirators.pdf

27 Government Exhibit: Philly Meeting - 15, 3:04-CR-240-G, U.S. v. HLF, et al., at 2,3, at http://www.txnd.uscourts.gov/judges/hlf2/09-29-08/Philly%20Meeting%2015.pdf

28 Steven Merley, "The Muslim Brotherhood in the United States," *Research Monographs on the Muslim World*, Series No 2, Paper No 3 (Hudson Institute, Washington, DC, April 2009), Appendix II, 52.

29 "List of Unindicted Co-conspirators and/or Joint Venturers," *United States of America v. Holy Land Foundation for Relief and Development, Attachment A*, in the online library of the NEFA Foundation, pp 1-11, accessed September 8, 2010, http://www.nefafoundation.org/miscellaneous/HLF/US_v_HLF_Unindicted_Coconspirators.pdf

30 Andrew C. McCarthy, "The Government's Jihad on *Jihad*," *The National Review Online*, May 13, 2008, accessed September 8, 2010, http://www.nationalreview.com/articles/224461/governments-jihad-i-jihad-i/andrew-c-mccarthy

31 Patrick Poole, "Willful Blindness: Army Unprepared for Another Jihadist Attack," May 3, 2010, http://pajamasmedia.com/blog/willful-blindness-army-unprepared-for-another-jihadist-attack

32 Accessed August 28th, 2010, http://www.defense.gov/news/d20100820FortHoodFollowon.pdf

33 *Ibid.*

34 "Ahmadinejad: Israel must be wiped off map," *Gulf Times* (Qatar), October 27, 2005 (http://www.gulf-times.com/site/topics/article.asp?cu_no=2&item_no=58372&version=1&template_id=37&parent_id=17).

35 The White House, Office of the Press Secretary, Remarks by John O. Brennan, Assistant to the President for Homeland Security and Counterterrorism—As Prepared for Delivery: "A New Approach to Safeguarding Americans," *Center for Strategic and International Studies*, James S. Brady Press Briefing Room, Washington, DC, August 6, 2009.

36 "Counterterror Adviser Defends Jihad as 'Legitimate Tenet of Islam,'" *Fox News*, May 27, 2010.

37 al-Misri, *Reliance of the Traveler*, , (Chapter o9.0), "Jihad," 599.

38 "Backgrounder: The President's Quotes on Islam," *News and Policies/Policies in Focus*, the White House, http://merln.ndu.edu/MERLN/PFIraq/archive/wh/islam1.pdf

39 "Remarks by the President on Strengthening Intelligence and Aviation Security," The White House, Office of the Press Secretary, January 7th, 2010, accessed April 29th, 2010, http://www.whitehouse.gov/the-press-office/remarks-president-strengthening-intelligence-and-aviation-security

40 Gary DeMary, "America's 200-Year War with Islamic Terrorism: The Strange Case of the Treaty of Tripoli" ;2009, http://www.americanvision.org/mediafiles/americas-200-year-old-war-with-islam.pdf

41 See Major Hasan's Power Point presentation at JihadWatch.org: http://www.Jihadwatch.org/images/MAJ%20Hasan%20Slides.pdf

42 Former Joint Chiefs of Staff expert Stephen Coughlin modified an existing briefing to show the fidelity of Major Hasan's presentation to sharia. On Hasan's acceptability as am "acting" substitute for the Fort Hood Imam based on that imam's assessment, see http://abcnews.go.com/video/playerIndex?id=9013819 accessed September 27, 2010.

43 Robert Spencer, "Islamic Radical Tied to New Boston Mosque," *Jihad Watch*, March 9, 2004, accessed August 5, 2010, http://www.jihadwatch.org/2004/03/islamic-radical-tied-to-new-boston-mosque.html

44 Explanatory Memorandum

45 "Criminal Complaint, United States of America vs. Abdurahman Mohammed Alamoudi, United States District Court, Eastern District of Virginia", September 2003, accessed April 29, 2010, http://fl1.findlaw.com/news.findlaw.com/hdocs/docs/terrorism/usalamoudi93003cmp.pdf

46 al-Misri, *Reliance of the Traveler*, h8.17, 272.

47 al-Misri, '*Reliance of the Traveler*, ol.2, 583-84 enumerates those categories of Muslims who "are not subject to retaliation" for killing: "(4) a father or mother (or their fathers or mothers) for killing their offspring, or offspring's offspring."

48 al-Misri, *Reliance of the Traveler*, m10.4, 538. See also Quran Sura 4:34: "....And to those women on whose part ye fear disloyalty and ill-conduct, admonish them (first), (next) refuse to share their beds, (and last) beat them...."

49 al-Misri, *Reliance of the Traveler*, o4.3: "Circumcision is obligatory (for both men and women…...for women, removing the prepuce of the clitoris…)."

50 Quran Sura 4:3: "...marry women of your choice, two, or three, or four..."

51 Mohammed ibn Isma'il Bukhari, *The Translation of the Meaning of Sahih al-Bukhari*, trans. Mohammed Muhsin Khan, 8 vols. (Medina, Dar al-Fikr: 1981) 5:58.234

52 al-Misri, *Reliance of the Traveler*, m3.7, 520.

53 al-Misri, *Reliance of the Traveler*, m5.1, 525.

54 al-Misri, *Reliance of the Traveler*, ol.2, pgs. 583-84 enumerates those categories of Muslims who "are not subject to retaliation" for killing: "(4) a father or

mother (or their fathers or mothers) for killing their offspring, or offspring's offspring."

55 Quran Sura 2:233: "Your wives are as a tilth unto you, so approach your tilth when or how ye will...."

56 Maxim Lott, "Advocates of Anti-sharia Measures Alarmed by Judge's Ruling," *Fox News*, August 5, 2010. Accessed August 6, 2010, http://www.foxnews.com/us/2010/08/05/advocates-anti-sharia-measures-alarmed-judges-ruling/

57 Imran Ahsan Khan Nyazee, *Theories of Islamic Law: The Methodology of Ijtihad.*, 2d ed., (Kuala Lumpur: The Other Press, 2002), 50. For example, from a contemporary Pakistani law professor:

> Islam, it is generally acknowledged, is a "complete way of life" and at the core of this code is the law of Islam. This implies that a Muslim through his submission to Islam not only accepts the unity of Allah, the truth of the mission of Mohammed, but also agrees through a contract (*bay'ah*) with the Muslim community that his life be regulated in accordance with the *ahkam* of Allah, and in accordance with these *ahkam* alone. No other sovereign or authority is acceptable to the Muslim, unless it guarantees the application of these laws in their entirety. Any other legal system, howsoever attractive it may appear on the surface, is alien for Muslims and is not likely to succeed in the solution of their problems; it would be doomed from the start. ... A comprehensive application of these laws, which flow directly or indirectly from the decrees (*ahkam*) of Allah, would mean that they should regulate every area of life, from politics to private transactions, from criminal justice to the laws of traffic, from ritual to international law, and from the laws of taxation and finance to embezzlement and white collar crimes.

58 Jerrold M. Post, *Leaders and their Followers in a Dangerous World: The Psychology of Political Behavior*, (Cornell University Press: Ithaca, NY, 2004), 139, citing Amir Taheri, *Holy Terror*, (unknown binding, 1989).

> "It is the nature of Islam to dominate, not to be dominated, to impose its law on all nations and to extend its power to the entire planet."

59 Andrew Bostom, "Shiite Iran's Genocidal Jew-Hatred: Part 3," accessed August 6, 2010, http://www.andrewbostom.org/blog/2008/07/20/390/

60 Jason Burke and Ian Traynor, "Fears of an Islamic Revolt in Europe Begin to Fade," *The Guardian Observer*, July 26, 2009, accessed July 4, 2010,

http://www.guardian.co.uk/world/2009/jul/26/radicalisation-european-muslims

61 Sayyid Qutb, *Milestones*, (Salimiah, Kuwait: International Islamic Federation of Student Organizations, 1978 [written 1966]), 139.

62 Majid Khadduri, *War and Peace in the Law of Islam*, (Baltimore, 2006), 64. See also Andrew Bostom, *The Legacy of Jihad* (Amherst, NY: Prometheus, 2005), 95-6.

63 Siddiqi, Methodology of Dawah Ilallah, 57.

64 See the Mapping Sharia Project at https://www.mappingsharia.us

65 See The Investigative Project on Terrorism, directed by Steven Emerson, for a voluminous collection of the Holy Land Foundation trial documents at http://www.investigativeproject.org

66 Accessed September 9, 2010, http://www.shoebat.com/bio.php

67 Accessed September 9, 2010, http://www.kamalsaleem.com/

68 Accessed September 9, 2010, http://www.ignatius.com/Products/SOH-H/son-of-hamas.aspx

69 Nyazee, *Theories of Islamic Law: The Methodology of Ijtihad*, 118, 119, 318, 316.

70 Amir Taheri, *Holy Terror: Inside the World of Islamic Terrorism* (Adler & Adler, 1987), 241-3.

Made in the USA
Middletown, DE
30 July 2016